THE WEAK STRONGMAN

SAMSON

By Marilyn Lashbrook

Illustrated by Chris Sharp

ME TOO!
R E A D E R S

ROPER PRESS, INC.
DALLAS, TEXAS

ME TOO! READERS are designed to help you share the joy of reading with children. They provide a new and fun way to improve a child's reading skills- by practice and example. At the same time, you are teaching your child valuable Bible truths.

THE WEAK STRONGMAN presents several important truths needed by today's children. Through Samson's life they will learn that external strength and beauty, so valued by the world, cannot make us into happy successful persons. Children will be challenged to obey their parents, to learn self-control, to honor God's Word and strengthen themselves on the inside as well as the outside.

Reading is key to successful education. Obeying the principles of God's Word opens the door to a successful life. ME TOO! READERS encourage your children in both!

Bold type: Child reads
Regular type: Adult reads
⬢ : Wait for child to respond
❤❤ : Talk about it!

Library of Congress Catalog Card Number: 90-60456
ISBN 0-86606-442-7

Art direction and design by
Chris Schechner Graphic Design

THE WEAK STRONGMAN

SAMSON

By Marilyn Lashbrook

Illustrated by Chris Sharp

Taken from Judges 13-16

ME TOO!
R E A D E R S

"We're going to have a baby!" said Mrs. Manoah to her husband. "An angel told me so!"

Manoah was excited. He and his wife did not have any children.

"The angel told me our baby will be set apart to God," Mrs. Manoah said. "He even told me not to cut our son's hair!"

Manoah prayed, "Oh God, I beg you to send the man of God to teach us how to raise our child." Manoah wanted to be a good father.

God heard his prayer and the Angel of
the Lord returned. But there were no
magic answers for raising an obedient
child. Parents can only do their best. God
helps too. But each child makes his
own choices.

Manoah and his wife planned and dreamed while they waited for their little son to come. At last, the baby was born. The man and woman finally had a child to hug and kiss. They called him Samson, which means "sunlight." And baby Samson

brightened their lives and brought
happiness to their home.

**They laughed as he gurgled and cooed.
They smiled when he wiggled and kicked.
Manoah and his wife loved to watch their
little Sunbeam grow and change.**

Every day Samson grew a little bigger
and a little stronger. God's Spirit began to
work in his heart. And Samson's parents
loved their son and taught him God's laws.

But as Samson grew older, he did not listen to his parents or obey their teaching. Their ways seemed old fashioned. Samson wanted his own way. He exercised his body, but he did not exercise his soul by obeying God's laws.

So even though Samson grew stronger on the outside, he grew weaker on the inside. The more he ignored his parents, the more difficult it was for him to gather the strength to do the right things.

On the outside, Samson was mightier than any other man. People admired his strong body...but they did not like his weak will. God had given Samson arms that could lift the heaviest loads. He could fight the wildest animals. He could knock down the biggest trees.

But Samson choose not to control his
temper,
or keep secrets,
or tell the truth,
or say "No!" to himself.

Samson had to have whatever he
wanted, even if it were bad for him. Each
wrong choice left him weaker on the inside.

In fact, if Samson were not stronger on
the outside than he was on the inside, he
would have been too weak to wrestle
a cricket.

One day, when Samson was old enough to date, he saw a beautiful Philistine girl. Her face was enchanting, but she did not have the love of God in her heart.

A good wife needs a lot more than a pretty face. But Samson didn't care. He wanted to marry this Philistine girl.

The Philistines were enemies. They were cruel to the people of Israel. Samson was born to protect his people from the Philistines. And now, he wanted to marry one of them.

"Why can't you find a girl from our country?" asked his parents. They loved him and wanted him to marry a girl who would obey God. But Samson would not listen.

So Samson's parents went with him to Philistia to meet the girl. While they were there, Samson took a walk through a vineyard. Suddenly a roaring lion jumped in his path.

Samson had no weapon, but he did not run away. He fought the lion with his bare hands. God gave Samson the strength to kill the lion.

Then Samson married his Philistine girl friend. He thought he would be happy.

But she lied to him. She cried to get what she wanted. She double crossed him. And while he was away visiting his parents she married another man.

Samson was angry! He wanted to get even with all the Philistine people.

He caught three hundred foxes and fastened torches to their tails. They ran through the Philistines' fields, setting fire to the grain. Soon all the crops were destroyed.

Samson's people were afraid. They thought the Philistines would start a war. "Let's turn Samson over to the enemy," they said.

So three thousand men from his own country tied him up and took him to the Philistines. But Samson flexed his muscles. The ropes broke and fell to the ground.

Then Samson grabbed a jawbone of an donkey and started swinging it. He killed three thousand Philistines that day.

Now the enemies were afraid of Samson! They stayed away from the people of Israel. God used Samson to protect Israel.

One day, Samson saw another beautiful Philistine woman named Delilah. Delilah did not love God or obey His laws. But Samson wanted her. Had Samson learned his lesson? ⬤

Even though the woman was bad for him, Samson wanted her. And he was still too weak inside to say "No" to himself.

Then, when Samson was away, his enemies came to see Delilah. They offered her a lot of money if she would help them. "Find out the secret of Samson's strength," they said, "then tell us so we can capture him."

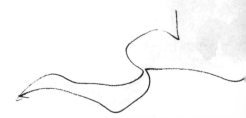

When Samson came, Delilah snuggled up to him. "You are so strong," she said,"What is your secret?"

Samson was not strong enough on the inside to say, "No, I will NOT tell you!" So he lied. "If anyone ties me with seven fresh bow strings, I'll be as weak as any man," Samson told her.

When Samson went to sleep, Delilah tied his hands with seven fresh bow strings. Then she woke him up. Snap! Off popped the strings!

"You lied to me!" Delilah pouted. "Now, tell me how you can be captured!"

Again and again Samson lied to her. No matter what Delilah tried, Samson easily escaped. But Delilah didn't give up. Day after day she cried and begged. Samson grew tired of her nagging and finally told her what she wanted to know.

"My hair has never been cut," he said, "I am a Nazarite. I am set apart to God. If my head were shaved, my strength would leave me."

Now you would think a person would learn after a while. But Samson couldn't keep his mouth shut. He had to tell.

You can guess what happened, can't you?

Delilah had Samson's head shaved.
When he woke up, he had no strength. The
Philistines grabbed him and poked out his
eyes. The they chained him in prison and
made him push a grindstone.

The days passed and Samson's hair grew back.

One day, the Philistines were celebrating. They brought Samson out of prison to perform for them. "Let me feel the pillars that hold up the building,"

Samson said to a servant. "I need to lean on them."

There were about three thousand people in the building watching Samson. And Samson wanted to get even with them for blinding him. At last, Samson prayed to God, "Lord make me strong one more time so I can avenge my enemies."

Do you think Samson should have started praying sooner? ⬣ What kind of strength did Samson need most? ⬣

Samson held his breath and tightened his muscles. He pushed with all his might. The building shook. The pillars gave way. And the roof came crashing down on all the people.

Justice was done. The people who blinded Samson were dead. The enemies of God's people had been punished.

But Samson was dead too. His strong body lay crushed beneath the pillars.

Samson thought it enough,
To be outwardly strong,
But deep in his heart,
He was awfully wrong.
If only he'd prayed,
and said "No!" to sin,
He'd have lived a long life,
The strongest of men. ❤❤

ME TOO!
B O O K S

For Ages 2-5

SOMEONE TO LOVE
THE STORY OF CREATION

TWO BY TWO
THE STORY OF NOAH'S FAITH

"I DON'T WANT TO"
THE STORY OF JONAH

"I MAY BE LITTLE"
THE STORY OF DAVID'S GROWTH

"I'LL PRAY ANYWAY"
THE STORY OF DANIEL

WHO NEEDS A BOAT?
THE STORY OF MOSES

"GET LOST LITTLE BROTHER"
THE STORY OF JOSEPH

THE WALL THAT DID NOT FALL
THE STORY OF RAHAB'S FAITH

NO TREE FOR CHRISTMAS
THE STORY OF JESUS' BIRTH

"NOW I SEE"
THE STORY OF THE MAN BORN BLIND

DON'T ROCK THE BOAT!
THE STORY OF THE MIRACULOUS CATCH

OUT ON A LIMB
THE STORY OF ZACCHAEUS

ME TOO!
R E A D E R S

For Ages 5-8

IT'S NOT MY FAULT
MAN'S BIG MISTAKE

GOD, PLEASE SEND FIRE!
ELIJAH AND THE PROPHETS OF BAAL

TOO BAD, AHAB!
NABOTH'S VINEYARD

THE WEAK STRONGMAN
SAMSON

Available at your local
bookstore
or from
Roper Press
915 Dragon Street
Dallas, Texas 75207
1-800-284-0158